D0065164

DON'T DIE
Waiting to Be Brave

Andrea T. Goeglein, PhD

SERVINGSUCCESS®

Contents

Dedication

This book is dedicated to the bravest people I know,

my Mom and Dad,

Christina and Andrew Terzano.

Thank you for teaching me what real love is.

With Deep Gratitude

It is traditional to have an acknowledgments page in a book wherein the author thanks all those who helped make the book possible. I have always thought those pages were odd. For me, it's not about acknowledging people for their contributions to the book. Instead, I want to express my deep gratitude for the part they played in the development of my soul, which is nothing less than the journey of my life's work.

From that perspective, I want to acknowledge how deeply grateful I am for the people who hurt me—or, to be more precise, the people I perceive to have hurt me. The pain of transforming the perceived hurt set me on a mission to create the life of gratitude I strive for each day.

Some gratitude can never be deep enough. That is how I feel about Vincent Crowder. Vincent, you came into my life synchronistically and you saved my life synchronistically. Thank you.

I am grateful for my cousin, Gary Russo. A synchronistic period of his life allowed me to reunite with him and refine my work through the joy he was experiencing. Telling his story will remain a centerpiece of my moment-by-moment learnings and teachings. #RIPSecondAveSinatra

I am grateful for Katherine Armstrong. She came into my life as an editor; she will be in my life forever as a friend. Katherine, our work together has helped my spirit grow in ways I could not have imagined.

I am grateful for being born a Catholic and for the Catholic Church. When you are good, you are very, very good. And when you are not, I am grateful for the forgiveness you teach me.

I am grateful to Philip Nix for gifting me his conceptualization of finding your voice as only the first step to minding your voice.

I am grateful to Dovetail Publishing Services for their creativity in design, Deb McKew for her editorial support, and Marianne Wallace for her detailed eye, and also to each of the early draft readers for their insight. Each in your own way helped me refine my story until I believed that in telling it I would be helping others refine and tell their stories. Thank you.

Dana Christina Goeglein-Courtney-Rizer, you are my true "rite of passage." Deep gratitude does not even come close! I will never be able to adequately express the depth of my love for you.

I will be forever grateful that Richard Goeglein entered my life, transformed my life, and has been with me for every step on our crooked road of life success. You are my partner in knowing that love is stronger than death.

Be Brave,
Andrea 10/2/15

Don't Die™ Principles

Change Your Awareness and
Your Perspective Changes.

You Teach What You Need to Learn.

You Can Make Excuses
or You Can Achieve Your Goals,
but You Cannot Do Both.

Experience Is What You Get When
You Don't Get What You Want.

What step would I take today if I were brave?

—Jana Stanfield

Welcome

If this is your first time reading a Don't Die™ book, welcome. If you have read any of the other books in the series, welcome back.

Let me be clear about something from the beginning:

Don't Die books are not about death and dying!

Don't Die books are about the synchronistic nature of life, love, trust, gratitude, forgiveness and the crooked road of success; specifically, they are an opportunity for you to experience *your* life as a success. *Don't Die* books help you understand that a lifetime devoted to exploring those qualities in your life will help ensure that you are living your spirit today and that your spirit will never die as long as *you* keep it alive. They show how you can bring to life each of these ideas by remembering the four *Don't Die* Principles on page ix.

Don't Die Waiting to Be Brave, the third book in the series, is about being brave enough to love yourself enough to finally go after what you want out of life. To recognize that your life really matters, that who and how you love really matters, and that you are successful. When you take the step to say all this about your life, you will have proven to yourself that you are brave!

That is it in a nutshell. Your bravery. Your life. Your loves. Your success.

I will start by being brave enough to acknowledge that I am teaching what I need to learn about the nature of both waiting and being brave. We think we are waiting for something to happen so the next positive opening will occur in our lives. What we are really waiting for is to break loose of our resistance to what is. I had been waiting over two years for the right story of life, love and success to come into my life so I could write this book. Then something changed or maybe a lot of somethings changed. Toward the end of 2014, I came to realize that the true story I had been waiting to write is the story of life itself, and that the only way I could authentically write

> *What we are really waiting for is to break loose of our resistance to what is.*

that story was to make it the story of my life. Problem was, I was still working up the courage to admit that to myself.

I had been waiting for some extraordinary in-the-moment story of someone else's sensational, synchronistic transformation that propelled them to their next level of life success. I was waiting for just the right time, just the right person, just the right everything. And it did not happen. Slowly, very slowly, it became clear why.

I am a lifelong adrenaline junkie who was still waiting for the happy ending instead of seeing the happy *being*. Sure, I teach that love is all there is, yet I kept waiting for more. Sure, I teach gratitude and the value of being present in the moment, yet I kept suspecting there was more in the next moment. Then it came to me. The "more" I was missing wasn't a sensational event. There was no crisis, giant leap forward or "aha moment." It was more like a million points of light coming together so I could finally see. I recognized that all the bravery that lined my life—and everyone's life—in the ordinary moments adds up to an extraordinary, successful life.

Don't Die Waiting to Be Brave is the story of these ordinary points of bravery, the synchronistic moments we all engage in, and the transformative power of minding our voices, forgiving, trusting, and learning to love ourselves and our lives, while we wait.

I grew brave enough to share and use my own story. Brave enough to recognize that the mere act of telling this story took extraordinary courage. That was all I had to be, brave *enough*.

When will you be brave enough to recognize your story?

Don't Die Principle

*Change Your Awareness
and Your Perspective Changes.*

We think we're waiting for something to happen so the next positive opening will occur in our lives. What we're really waiting for is to break loose from our resistance to what *is*. That's where bravery comes in. Awareness of waiting allows us to change our perspective and accept that what we do *while* we wait—while we live our dash— is defining our lives and what we achieve.

Don't Die Waiting
to Be Brave Enough

Being brave doesn't mean you can't feel afraid. It means you have the courage to step beyond your fears and do it anyway.

—Cathy Pagano

When Will You Be Brave Enough?

"When will you be brave enough?"

As my lunch guest spoke these words, I froze. We were having such a nice time, why did he have to go and spoil the experience with something so true?

The year was 1996 and I was knee-deep into collecting, analyzing and researching my dissertation topic: exploring the moral development of transformational CEOs. I had arranged lunch on this particular day with the Chief Ethics Officer for a huge New York City-based investment banking firm. I know what you are thinking. What investment banking firms have a Chief Ethics Officer? The wild economic ride of the 1980s, culminating with the stock market crash that became known as Black Monday, had ushered in an economic recession and the major corporate layoffs of the early 1990s. By the time of the lunch in question, the Internet was born and the undercurrents in the financial markets were flowing yet again, but now with deep ethical wounds of distrust.

The distrust started with bonds called "junk" and ended with the death of the dream of lifetime job security born in the 1950s post-war boom. Corporate training rooms were filled with workshops that encouraged employees to view themselves as employed by "You, Inc." Unknowingly, companies were sending the message: "You better trust yourself because you can no longer trust us."

My research was taking place against this backdrop—a backdrop that was changing faster than any respectable set designer could envision. As I was discussing my preliminary findings with my lunch guest, I innocently said, "The research is trending in the right direction, but without the ability to measure the spiritual nature of a CEO I feel like I am leaving out the biggest part of the investigation."

In the next moment, he looked up from his soup—soup I was paying for—and lobbed the now infamous question, "When will you be brave enough?"

Of course, my immediate response was "Brave enough for what?" to which he retorted, "Brave enough to follow up on that instinctual part of your investigation."

That was actually easy to answer. Or so I thought. I didn't need bravery. I needed completion according to plan. I was, and still am, a very logical, step-by-step thinker. I wanted to finish my doctorate and get back to working and making money. I did not want to invest my money and life energy into changing a system of business based in logic—one that I already knew was resistant to merging the proven with the impossible to prove. That was not a lesson I wanted to learn or to teach.

———•◆•———

Keeping the questions alive doesn't mean deciding what's true. It just means keeping the conversation engaged.

—Elizabeth Lloyd Mayer

Fast forward twenty years and I can now answer the question "When will you be brave enough?" in a very different way. Why? Because I have come to understand that being brave is not a single moment in time. I have come to *live* this truth, too. Being brave is about the everyday points of bravery that when taken together and viewed from a collective perspective make for an extraordinary life of love. Being brave is taking the time to view a life from a moment-by-moment perspective and realizing that a life of love is the ultimate life of success.

As I look back, my inability to pursue the question in 1996 was not truly based on my espoused desire to finish school. That was just an excuse. I didn't explore the intuitive and spiritual aspect of leadership and personal transformation at that time because I would not have understood what I was studying. I would have been studying something I had not yet learned! I wasn't ready to teach what I needed to learn (there's that *Don't Die* Principle again). Some learning takes a long time to make you brave enough to become the teacher.

Being brave is not a single moment in time.

In 1996, all I understood was that business and success were about finding logical solutions. In fact, I saw *all of life* as a problem to be solved. I only knew how to study from within my head; in fact, I only knew how to live life from within my head. Back then I would have set out to prove that intuition and spiritual self-awareness were critical aspects of transformational leading and leadership. The words love and success could not have been linked for me then.

It took several decades more for me to understand that all questions—whether about life or the business of life—need to be explored from my heart and then embraced by my head. Today, I know that intuition, spiritual self-awareness, love and success are important parts of business because they are central to all of life. The heart does not prove anything. Instead it has the capacity to expand our logic and, therefore, opportunities in ways we can't even imagine.

It has taken my whole life thus far to see how being brave enough to hold on to a question, brave enough to never stop looking for answers, and brave enough to take action even when I didn't know the right answer, was as brave as I needed to be to succeed and to succeed with love. It has taken my whole life thus far and every manifestation of my spirit—from scared little kid, to striving young adult, to inexperienced business owner, to uninitiated corporate wife and overscheduled mother, to author and life catalyst—to see that when I am brave enough, the love shows up to carry me through.

Intuition, spiritual self-awareness, love and success are important parts of business.

The Fastest Dash

Many people die with their music still in them. Why is this so? Too often it is because they are always getting ready to live. Before they know it, time runs out.

—Oliver Wendell Holmes, Sr.

I started this book by saying it was not about death and dying, and it is not. This book is about encouraging you to see how brave you are. More specifically, it's about how to be brave enough to "live your dash."

What on earth does that mean? Let me explain.

Just about the same year my lunch guest was enjoying his soup and questioning my bravery, author Linda Ellis was inspired to write a poem entitled "The Dash." Over the decades since, tens of millions of people have been touched by the poem's simple concept that your life is represented not by your date of birth or date of death, but by the *dash* between those dates.

If all goes well, you will be 80 soon. The hard thing to understand about that dash is how quick living that dash feels. I hate to break it to you, but no matter your age, if all goes well, you will be 80 soon.

Nothing helps us live in the moment better than realizing that the moments we have left to live are fewer than the ones we have lived so far. Just ask an 80-year-old! When talking about his book, *Unforgettable*, National Public Radio journalist Scott

11

Simon shared a lesson he learned from his mother as she neared the end of her life. Scott quoted her saying: "You know, honey, you ought to spend more time talking to people in their 80s . . . They have looked right across the street at death for more than a decade, and they know what's really important in life."[1]

What's really important? Yikes. That's not a question I like to answer on a daily basis. Why? Because I usually get worried that I'm investing my time in the wrong places.

Stating that I "usually get worried" actually understates the amount of time I historically invested in worrying, especially about whether I would ever achieve success! The poem on the next page, which I free-wrote for an exercise in a leadership training class, captures my thinking at that time.

I wish I could say that after I wrote that poem I had a major breakthrough and stopped worrying about time, success and whether I would ever have enough time to achieve the success I desired. Like everyone else, I am "time-gap" challenged.

In reality, no matter how hard you try, you cannot accurately imagine how fast you will be 10 years older or 20 years older, or how soon you will be 80. Why? Many research studies have examined the gap between chronological age and a person's psychological impression of their age. The answer they came to: we tend to "feel" younger than our actual age.

We tend to "feel" younger than our actual age.

That's why it's so critically important to focus on the moment-by-moment. If you stay in the moment, you know what's important *right now*. You know that what comes next will be equally important when you get there.

Success*

I am going to write a poem about success.
Success that brings smiles, success that brings joy.
Success that brings rewards that seem so out of
    reach before success comes.
When will success be the now instead of the future?
When will success be the doing and not the done?
When will success be?
When I am willing, success will come.
Because when I am willing I will see that success is
    now.
It is where I have traveled and how I have traveled,
    not where I have yet to travel.
Success is.
I must let it be.

Andrea T. Goeglein, PhD
March 27, 2001

*A.T. Goeglein, *Success*, 2001. May be used without permission as
long as full and complete attribution is stated as: *Success*, Andrea T.
Goeglein, PhD, all rights reserved, www.ServingSuccess.com

Picture Perfect

Mother's Day 1986 started out picture perfect. Just look at these two happy kids: Matthew and our daughter Dana. Who wouldn't want to be them?

My awareness of that afternoon is as clear to me now as it was then. It was a hot, sunny Southern day. Friends had brought their son over for a lazy afternoon by the pool. The mom, a gourmet chef, had prepared a feast that we had all enjoyed. Being good parents and rule-followers, we had held the kids out of the water after lunch for the appropriate amount of time. Then my husband Richard jumped in to play with them for a while before making an early exit to get ready for a business trip. Nothing could have been more normal. And nothing could have prepared me for what happened next.

As my friends and I lounged at the pool's edge waiting for the kids to get tuckered out, the happy, rambunctious little Matthew began to rock the raft. Have you ever counted how long it takes to say, "Don't do that!" One second. One second. Did you get that? One second. Well, I don't need to tell you that one second was not enough to stop the raft from toppling over plunging the two children deep into the 12-foot end of the pool.

Instinctively and without thought, I jumped in, as did Matthew's father. Within seconds I had hold of Dana and swam to the top. But I had overlooked one small detail. I didn't know how to swim, let alone know how to save someone. In the time it took for me to remember that essential truth, we sank—this time together.

Somehow I managed to get us back to the surface again. In the periphery of my vision, I noticed Matthew and his dad

15

on the edge, already to safety. Then, we were swallowed by the pool again. Just like the first time, I got us up to the surface, but I couldn't keep us up there and get us out. Down we sank, together but floundering, moving further away from the surface and life-saving air.

What happened next as I struggled in vain against gravity? I started to think. Yes, think. I consciously recalled the adage about drowning: you have only three attempts to be saved. If that was true, I had already used up two of the three attempts to save Dana. So I did what I knew how to do best at that time in my life: I made a decision. I decided I was not going to let her go down. I decided to succeed in getting us to the top and keeping us there, delivering Dana to safety. And I decided that if she went down, I would go down with her. I made this rational decision while frantically attempting to get us back to the surface.

As I broke into the air, I saw Matthew's father's welcoming arms reaching for Dana. In the moments between my second and third attempts, he had realized we were in trouble. Once Dana was safely with him, I was free to reach for the pool's edge, saving myself.

Was I brave enough because I loved my daughter so much?

Or was I able to love so much because I was this brave?

Die to the past every moment. You don't need it. Only refer to it when it is absolutely relevant to the present. Feel the power of this moment and the fullness of Being.

—Echart Tolle

Don't Die Principle

You Teach What You Need to Learn.

Learning, like all of life, is a crooked path of connected events. Sometimes we don't even notice that seemingly unrelated occurrences offer different versions of the same lesson. Sometimes we are the student and sometimes we are the teacher. And often we are drawn to teach exactly what we need to learn. When we teach before we embody the lesson, we are not being disingenuous. We are simply taking the steps needed to keep us motivated to learn more.

Finding and Minding My Voice

Courage is what it takes to stand up and speak; courage is also what it takes to sit down and listen.

—Winston Churchill

Synchronicity

Synchronicity: the experience of two or more events that are causally unrelated occurring together in a meaningful manner.

It may come as a surprise to you that not all synchronistic events are pleasant. I find no definition of synchronicity that assigns moral meaning of right or wrong, good or bad. There does appear, however, to be a pop-culture attribution assigned to synchronicity which implies that synchronistic events herald some wonderful connection, filled with possibility for

> *Synchronistic events give us an opportunity for bravery.*

good outcomes. At an eternal level, that might be true. On a moment-by-moment or even decade-by-decade basis it may be difficult to ascertain connections, let alone deduce the meaning or assign a level of positivity to them.

Yet over the course of our lifetime those synchronistic events that throw us off our game or present challenges open doors to growth and experience that are ultimately positive. They give us an opportunity for bravery. They give us the opportunity to learn, then teach, then learn again.

It is only now, almost 45 years later, that I understand that minding my voice—a central element of bravery—began with a synchronistic event. A visiting priest in one church in 1966 helped me *find* my voice. That discovery started the process that culminated in my finally *minding* my voice—again in a church in reaction to yet another visiting priest in 2011. Part of that process involved my being humbled when I used my voice before I understood its true power.

Finding My Voice, 1966

 The year was 1966 and I was 10 years old. It was spring, the season of blooming. In the Catholic Church, spring is also the Easter season of renewal and resurrection. I sat dutifully in a pew with my childhood classmates at yet another mandatory church service. Attendance was proof that you were fulfilling your religious obligations. I'll admit that at that point in my life, I actually thought God was keeping track and that gave me great comfort. God and priests, His envoys on earth, knew everything that happened in my life.

This particular service included the Rite of General Absolution, which happened just once a year in the lead-up to Easter. The point was to make sure all wayward Catholics were generally absolved from their sins, and therefore ready to participate in the sacrament of the Holy Eucharist, before the end of the Lenten season. Of course, even as children we knew that the *general* absolution ought to be followed up with actually going to Confession where the priest would *really* absolve you of your sins.

A visiting priest happened to be officiating at this service. I didn't know him, but my heart will forever be filled with gratitude for the lesson he shared that day. I remember he was young; this has always stood out to me. I don't remember exactly what he said during his homily, but I do remember being inspired to action. I know it had to be about forgiveness.

I know it had to be about confirming that I was supported—by God, by the church, by my family—no matter what I had done.

I know that I trusted that priest.

How do I remember that I trusted him when I can't remember much else with any degree of accuracy? Because after the service I waited on *his* confessional line to share a secret that had been burning a hole in my young heart for years—a secret about something that had been happening since I was five years old.

By the time you're five, you have a lot of knowledge about right and wrong. You know who loves you. You know who you can trust to protect you. You know that a touch can bring great comfort. What you don't know is that there is a wrong kind of touching. That someone you care about and trust, and who you believe loves you, can hurt you and do an unfathomable amount of harm.

Unfortunately for more children than we like to admit, five is also an age when children get sexually abused.

He was a family protector. A high-ranking police officer. My dad's best friend. Even as a five-year-old, I knew that the bond of trust between our families was strong. With all that, how could what he was doing be a sin? How come he didn't want me to tell anyone, especially my parents?

Circumstances like the one I found myself in at such a young age can cause trusting children to turn into very untrusting adults. I, luckily, am not one of those people. Why?

Because that visiting priest gave me the confidence that I had done nothing wrong and convinced me to go home and talk to my parents immediately. He came into my life for one day, the day I found my voice and opened up the rest of my life to trust and love.

3 S's of Action

Show Up

Shut Up (listen)

Shine

From Arrogant to Articulate

 I know I'm not the only child told more than once by her mother, "Watch your tone with me, young lady." Truth be told, at my childhood home, any warning to "watch my tone" would have been quickly followed by a good swift kick in the you know-where. For much of my adolescence and young adulthood, "that tone" was the only voice I knew I had. I remember the first time "that tone" came back to haunt me enough to make me want to be brave enough to change it.

I prided myself in being one of the top ten 1974 graduates of a secretarial school that had a major conglomerate, W. R. Grace & Co., as its main sponsor. The honor of my rank came with a job offer there. During my initial meeting, I told the Human Resources executive that I had only one requirement: I would not work for a woman.

As you can guess, my first position was as secretary to one of the few, newly hired, female executives. One of my new boss's most recent job titles, prior to becoming the Senior Executive for Human Resources, was Stewardess. Oh, and Connecticut Neighbor to the CFO. Remember, it was 1974. Most nurses were female; most teachers were female; all secretaries were female; and most corporate executives were male. It had been 10 years since the enactment of the Civil Rights Act of 1964 and nine years since the launch of the Equal Employment Opportunity Commission (EEOC). By 1974 we had only just begun to see females in executive positions. In a large corporation with government contracts there was an urgency to

27

comply with EEOC quotas. It was not unheard of that a woman assumed a position for which she had no prior education or experience.

As part of this trend, my new boss didn't have the education or related work experience. But she was smart, energetic and a positive force to be reckoned with. She was given a chance to prove she could learn and she succeeded rapidly. In turn, she showed me the same reverence and opportunity. If she was taking on a new learning challenge, she shared the challenge with me. It was with that support that I attended my first EEOC meeting, which was led by a member of the board of directors of W. R. Grace.

We gathered in the company cafeteria and this giant of a man in his navy suit, white shirt and conservative tie explained how hard the company was working to find and attract competent female executives. He expressed his frustration in not being able to "find" or "'reach" women to inform them that the company had lots of positions available and they were eager to fill them with women. The company, he explained, wanted to fulfill its EEOC quotas and was committed to its "promote from within" policy, but you can't promote people if they don't apply. My inside voice ("that tone") was sarcastically summarizing his remarks as, "Darn those women. How dare you give this company that much trouble?" What my outside voice said was not very different.

Filled with the encouragement of my incredible boss and the bravado of an 18-year-old from Queens, I raised my hand. When formally recognized to speak, I stood up and said something to the effect of, "I don't know why it is so hard to find us. Why don't you post the jobs on the bulletin board in the ladies room? We go there several times a day." I sat back down. I don't remember the giant blue-suited executive saying much of anything other than politely thanking me for my contribution.

Until the next day. It seems his outside voice was saying thank you, but his inside voice was fuming. The day after our group meeting my super-supportive boss called me into her office and closed the door. I sat down again. With as much compassion as she could muster, my boss told me what I did was wrong. It wasn't that my idea wasn't great. She actually thought it was brilliant in its simplicity. What was wrong was the delivery. My idea wouldn't succeed because of the tone. "Do you want to be known as arrogant or as someone who is articulate and who can influence others?" she asked. I knew the right answer. My voice, in its youth and arrogance, had labeled me a troublemaker not a problem solver. What I did not know then, but I know now after having learned how to mind my voice: arrogance does not equal bravery.

The Door to Forgiveness, Cathedral of Santiago de Compostela, as visited during my Camino de Santiago pilgrimage, October 2015.

Minding My Voice, 2011

"Father, please stop speaking."
"Father, please stop speaking."
"Father, please stop speaking."

Surprisingly, my voice was calm and steady as I stood and repeated those words until he did stop speaking. Moments before, the church was as hushed as expected when a priest is delivering his post-Gospel homily.

On this day, Monday, September 5, 2011, the words of that homily, rolling authoritatively from the old priest's mouth, were nothing short of shocking to me. Since the priest was not a regular officiator at the church, I assumed he was a visiting priest. At first I thought I was simply misunderstanding what he was saying, so I began to listen closer, as you do when you think you misheard something.

I leaned in and concentrated, glancing at my husband Richard to see if he was hearing what I was hearing. Richard raised his eyebrows, shook his head and began to pay closer attention, too. The priest's tirade was peppered with words admonishing anyone who voted democratic for going against God's will. In fact, he invocated "going against God's will" so many times I lost count. As the political lambasting continued inappropriately from the pulpit, I whispered in Richard's ear, "You can wait in the car. There is no reason for you to sit through this." His response revealed his familiar streak of dark humor, "Are you kidding? This is too hard to believe. I don't want to leave."

We kept sitting there, listening, shaking our heads. Somehow I became aware that the woman behind me was actually enthusiastically supporting the priest's every word. Keep in mind this wasn't a Southern Baptist or AME church with a tradition of "call back." This was a Catholic church, with Mass protocol, and Catholics don't "enthusiastically support" what the priest is saying. As I became increasingly uncomfortable, I found myself turning just enough to catch a glimpse of the woman. I wanted to see the face of the person who agreed with statements that were making my soul whisper "you cannot be quiet any longer." As best I could tell, she could have been anyone's 70+ grandmother, proudly wearing her American flag tee shirt to Labor Day Mass. While I would have assumed that she had learned a thing or two about Jesus and forgiveness over the years, she was clearly suffering amnesia of the heart. She had definitely forgotten any lessons about love she might ever have learned in church.

I kept wondering, "Where is the love in all this?"

Then in the middle of all my wondering, physical agitation and disbelief, I rose to my feet and slowly but audibly began my chant, "Father, please stop speaking."

I don't know how long it took for not only the priest, but also the entire church, to go dead silent. Time had stopped. Reflecting back, I know at that moment I was experiencing what Mihaly Csikszentmihalyi described as "flow—the state in which people are so involved in an activity that nothing else seems to matter."[2] I had a purpose and time had no meaning. I remember the astonished look on the old priest's face. He was visibly shocked, and to tell the truth, so was I. I really had no idea what would happen next, but I knew I had minded my voice.

Richard had an approving smirk on his face that read, "Oh, this is fun."

The fun began to end when a big-bellied security guard I had seen many times over the years appeared and asked me to leave. I confidently said he didn't have to worry, I was leaving. What happened next was somewhat surreal, more so than everything else up until that point. As Richard and I began to leave, people started yelling—some in agreement, some not.

Since I have a habit of sitting toward the front of a church, we had a long walk to exit that church. As we approached the midpoint of the aisle, eyes firmly on the door, I heard a voice, looked over, and paused the pace of our hasty exit. When I did, I realized many others were out of their seats and following us. I turned my attention back to the voice. It was an elderly African American woman saying, "Don't leave. Stay and fight." I recognized her face. She, too, was a regular attendee of Monday noon services. My heart broke for her because I knew she could not do what I had just done; she walked slowly and with assistance. She had to stay. I stopped just long enough to respond, "I did not come here to fight." That was my truth then and it is my truth now. I did not go to church that day to fight, and at the same time, I would no longer wait and be silent. I had minded my voice. I was no longer waiting to be brave enough to let it out.

Don't Die Principle

*You Can Make Excuses
or You Can Achieve Your Goals,
but You Cannot Do Both.*

You can make excuses or you can achieve your goals, but you cannot do both, at least not at the same time. If you find yourself saying you can't, you won't, or you don't know how to do something, yet you insist it is the very thing you want most, you are making excuses—excuses for not living the life you want.

Living the life you want is your ultimate responsibility. One of the biggest excuses we all seem to use comes from our unwillingness to take responsibility to forgive what we have done or what we have perceived has been done to us. By embracing forgiveness as a moment-by-moment responsibility you will be ready to stop making excuses and be brave enough to take action.

Forgiveness

. . . focusing on whatever we dislike empowers it.

—Ellen Debenport

3 N's of Responsibility

No Shame

No Blame

No Rationalization

The way to achieve forgiveness is to learn to explain every error you have made, or others have made, by telling the story using the 3 N's.

Forgiveness *Is* Self-Love

If finding my voice and minding my voice has taken most of my life, learning to forgive gave me back my voice—and my life!

Have you heard that you forgive someone not because it matters to them but because the act of forgiving a person (or external circumstance or institution) frees *you* to live a better life? That is exactly what it did for me and I wonder why it took me so long.

One reason is that forgiveness is self-love. When you forgive, you demonstrate that you love yourself more than you hate what another person did to you. You respect and value yourself enough to give yourself a renewed life. You are brave enough to risk upsetting others because you need freedom.

As a child and young adult, I knew nothing about the concept of self-love. I see now how much that held me back from full happiness—from truly living my dash. I was always waiting for something to break through. What I understand today is that we don't need to know everything in the first 25 years of life. But we should learn to love ourselves earlier in our lives—not from a false sense of entitlement or false self-esteem—but because doing so delivers enhanced opportunities to help others. We will do for others before we are willing to do for ourselves. That in part is why we learn to love others before we develop the skill to love ourselves. That is why it can take decades to forgive.

We should learn to love ourselves earlier in our lives.

11-24-93

Dear Andrea:

I received your letter and was very shocked. After reading it, I did something I have not done in a long time, I cried. To think that you could carry so much hate in your heart these many years. You were right, I did betray your trust and love but I did not do it intentionally. To hurt you would have been the last thing I would have intended. I loved you like my own daughter. I was very wrong in what I did and believe me I have regretted it ever happened all these years. I Had only myself to blame for my foolishness. I have carried the shame with me since it happened. I wish I could undo what happened but since that cannot be I can only ask you to forgive me.

Since moving to Florida I have changed my ways and have realized what I did in New York and believe me, it has not, and will not happen again. Too bad we did not move sooner before things went too far. I only ask you please if you can to remember the happy days in New York and to forgive me, please. I really am not the monster you described in your letter. I was weak, but I have overcome that weakness . At the time I just did not think of what I was doing. My judgement was poor because I was only thinking of my own satisfaction. I hope you can forgive me and try to erase from your heart the hate you feel for me. As I said, I never meant to hurt you in any way. ▆▆▆ and I have found a new life here in our old age, please don't try to destroy it. You would have nothing to gain but revenge and you would be hurting an innocent person ▆▆▆ who had no part in what I was responsible for.

My phone number is unlisted because of my son's debts. He owes so much money that we were being annoyed by his creditors.

Sincerely yours,

▆▆▆

Correspondence with the Past, 1993

 After years of debate with my therapist about why I felt dis-ease when I had such a good life, she put it on the table. "If you don't reach out to your abuser and say your piece, you will never find peace." Honestly, I thought she was the one who needed a shrink! Why on earth would I want to contact him? As she persisted, I recognized that I was so tired of feeling uneasy that I was willing to try anything as long as I had not tried it before. I was sick of doing the same thing over and over again (in this case therapy) and getting the same result. I was ready to stop making excuses and ready to live my life as a well-educated, happily married mother with work I enjoyed, outstanding health, and a large, loving extended family.

So I wrote a letter. I found my abuser's address. Because I didn't want him to be able to find me, I used a P.O. box in another city for the return address. I don't remember my letter being particularly hateful, but I do know I said my piece and then some.

Within days I got the response on the opposite page.

If I don't remember being hateful in my letter, I do remember that I hated his letter back. How could he write like that about something he did to a five-year-old? How could he give those excuses and then ask for my forgiveness? How could he implore me not to take revenge after what he had done?

After a few days Richard asked me what I was going to do. At first I said I didn't know and then it came to me. I would do nothing. I would be silent. I would not respond. Richard said that would be torture for my abuser; he would never know what I was going to do or when. I looked Richard in the eye and said, "Exactly."

Deciding to do nothing wasn't exactly revenge, but it wasn't forgiveness, either.

And a few more years passed. I continued to learn about forgiveness through my interest in spiritual and personal development. Yet I still wasn't feeling as great as I believed I should. And then it happened. I got it. While I had no idea if my silence was hurting him, I knew it was still hurting me. I synchronistically came across this quote by Sue Monk Kidd:

I learned a long time ago that some people would rather die than forgive. It's a strange truth, but forgiveness is a painful and difficult process. It's not something that happens overnight. It's an evolution of the heart.[3]

I typed the quote on a piece of paper, put it in an envelope and mailed it to him. I never heard from him again, and I never had a need to contact him again. I had stopped making excuses and I had achieved my goal. Living the life I wanted was my ultimate responsibility. Learning to forgive was my ultimate act of self-love.

Don't Die Principle

Experience Is What You Get When You Don't Get What You Want.

There are two words that people use when they don't want to be openly negative: "interesting" and "experience."

Ask a friend, "Did you like meeting your boyfriend's mother?" If she replies, "It was an interesting experience," settle in for a long conversation! Your friend didn't actually say something negative, but there's a big difference between saying "What an incredible woman!" and "It was an interesting experience."

Neutrally defined, experience is the skill or knowledge gained by personal observation of facts or events by which you are affected.[4] Whether the "experience" is positive or negative usually takes a lifetime—and a much broader perspective—to determine.

The experience of learning to forgive was not one I had set out to learn. I had trusted forgiveness would have a positive impact on my life long before I experienced that outcome.

Trust

Trust is the first step to love.

—Munshi Premchand

Only the Brave Need Apply

Yes, as Premchand wrote: "Trust is the first step to love,"[5] but it's not the only step. To live our dash, we take step after step, being hurt and then becoming brave enough to trust again, forgive again and love again.

No part of our lives gives us a better place to experience those steps than marriage or parenthood. These roles test and build our trust—trust in others and trust in ourselves—more than any others. I am convinced that they prove you are brave whether you know it or not. If you choose to take on both, you may not *feel* brave, but I can promise you will feel crazy at some point.

If you consciously choose to become a spouse or a parent, you are brave because you are taking on a lifetime commitment without even the slightest clue of the potential outcomes. One potential outcome is you'll have a lot of experiences you didn't want. No matter what, you can be sure that love gets you into these roles, and love must carry you through no matter what you experience. Not just love of the other, but love of yourself. And not just trust of the other, but trust in yourself.

Love gets you into these roles, and love must carry you through.

Trusting Myself

 Some girls want flowers and romance from their mate. I'm turned on by integrity and character. And I found them in an unlikely partner in a very unlikely place: a business meeting.

Richard Goeglein was our boss's boss. While I didn't like him initially, I remember the day I learned to respect him. He instructed me to assemble the secretarial staff in a conference room. I assumed it was to reprimand us for our unwillingness to work the excessive overtime being required during an acquisition. I was wrong.

I stood in the back of the room as he began to speak about how our work as secretaries fit into the big picture. Long before the cliché of quality circles had hit corporate America, he explained why what we were doing mattered. No one else had shown us so much respect or sought to inspire us. Richard showed that he valued us. Trusted us. And that we could trust him. I was attracted to him—to his *character*—immediately.

For the next four years I observed him. The character he exhibited in that meeting rarely faltered and when it did, his natural humor saved the day. By the time we started dating, I trusted him enough to tell him things I hadn't told anyone else. He didn't falter then either.

As a young woman it didn't dawn on me to find someone to complete me. It's not that I thought I was *that* good. It was the opposite: I had a huge amount of unworthiness (who would want to complete me?) and shame, and I had enough youthful

arrogance that I not only *could* take care of myself, I *would* take care of myself.

Richard was too busy living his own life to attempt to complete mine. Instead he gave me all the freedom and support I needed to take on that life journey for myself. To me, that's true love and that's what these photos represent to me. We shared a love for business and that connection gave me confidence. This confidence in my achievement—my "success" as I saw it then—came long before confidence in myself and, therefore, love of myself.

At 22, I didn't think of myself as brave for dating Richard. I knew the obvious: we shared a 21-year age difference. And I sure knew I was in love. What I didn't know was that I would lose some of my friends and the approval of my parents. Was I brave to marry someone given the age gap and lack of support from family? With hindsight, probably so, but not for the reasons you may think.

I was brave because I was willing to love, lose and trust that I would love and be loved again.

When marrying, ask yourself this question: Do you believe that you will be able to converse well with this person into your old age? Everything else in marriage is transitory.

—Friedrich Nietzsche

The Business of a Successful Marriage

About 30 years into our marriage, our daughter, Dana, asked us to share our thoughts about marriage. Here's what we wrote. The pictorial history referenced in the following letter is the source for many of the photographs in this book.

August 22, 2010

Dear Dana,

When you originally asked us to write you letters about love, marriage and life, we were both stymied. We were not sure what you wanted or needed us to share that had not already been shared or experienced. We also did not know what we could add separately that was not one of us just repeating what the other had already said.

We came to realize that at this point in our lives marriage is not a topic separate from us but rather a foundation that continues to support us. We needed to look back and show you where that foundation came from, why it was built the way it was, and why it still sustains us.

For us marriage started out as we think all marriages should. It was about physical attraction supported by shared values and dreams for the future. Over 30 years later it's not about "do we love each other?" but "because we love each other;" it is no longer about building a foundation based on our shared life values but rather depending on that foundation to support us no matter how many life earthquakes try to fracture the support beams.

What we have done is look back through a pictorial history of our union and selected those pictures that capture the key foundations of love, life and marriage. They remind us of where it all started and how come it has been built so strong.

You will have those pictures from the past and we hope that you feel our love in the present. As to the future, here are some tips we offer so your marriage can be as rich as ours has been.

1. You need to have a love of adventure. Marriage, like life, is not a trip you can really take the way you may have planned in your 20s. There are hints along the trail but no real map.
2. Build a foundation slowly from where you are moment-by-moment.
3. Be open to adding to that foundation.
4. Surround yourself with friends and family. And most of all, accept how that part of the foundation changes over time yet the parts that were added never leave you.
5. Have pets. They will love you when you think no one in the world does.
6. Children. If you choose to have children, do so because you want to give them life, not to complete yours. Accept your children even when they don't accept themselves—or you. Know that your only purpose is to teach them to create a legacy of love.

Most of all, laugh. Always find humor in all aspects of life. Fill your world with laughter, love the challenges as much as the pinnacles, and know God is present in you, with you, and because of you.

We love you.

Mom & Dad

No Experience Is the Right Experience

Your children are not your children. They are the sons and daughters of Life's longing for itself. They came through you but not from you and though they are with you yet they belong not to you.

—Khalil Gibran

 When we decided to have a child, I bought a book called *This Too Shall Pass*. It set to humor all that naturally happens in a pregnancy and the not-so-funny things that can happen when you become a parent. No matter the dilemma, the author always closed with the reminder, "This too shall pass!"

And pass it did—the toddler who didn't want to go to pre-school, the pain of a cross-country move, the dark decade of adolescence. The speed of living your dash is no clearer than when you reflect back on your life as a parent. What I have found is that in the blur of days that become years, and the years that become decades, being brave, forgiving, trusting and love are the only requirements for success.

Love from India

From: Dana Courtney [mailto:dana.gigs@gmail.com]
Sent: Thursday, February 6, 2014 3:23 AM
To: Andrea Goeglein
Subject: Love from India

Dear Mom,

Travel is such an amazing thing: We are constantly meeting new people in unfamiliar surroundings, and trying as best we can to get to know each other, create context, and share some part of our lives and ourselves in a relatively short span of time.

As I did this countless times this month with strangers who became fast friends, I wanted to share with you some of the memories, feelings, and realizations that arose about our relationship and you! (Don't be scared, it's nice. Read on).

Here are a few things I heard myself say to others as I talked about my growing up, my family and you:

1) You have thrown so many amazing parties in my lifetime. Birthday parties with personalized puff-painted shirts, pool parties with homemade guacamole, New Year's and Christmas parties filled with thoughtful surprises and real sparkle. You have always gone beyond to make these moments matter, and you have done all of this mostly thanklessly, in part because you like it, but more so because you love us. As I thought back on all those times and shared them with others, I wanted to

say thank you for providing me with countless celebrations and happy moments that made the most out of our family milestones and our time together.

2) Your encouragement and personal example are a huge part of why I'm on a spiritually guided path. I love you and thank you so much for this.

3) Our relationship has always been and continues to be one of the greatest sources of personal growth for me, and I am really grateful for your tireless love, patience and dedication to growth through every up and down we've ever experienced.

4) I have realized increasingly over time how often my words or actions must have hurt or deeply wounded you. For all of this, conscious and unconscious, in this lifetime and before, I'm sorry. Please forgive me.

I look forward to talking with you, seeing you and sharing more together soon. This time has been amazing, and I'm glad I'm headed home.

I love you so much.

D

Hastily sent from my iPhone.

The Camino de Santiago pilgrimage is also called The Way of St. James.
The way of the Camino is love.

Love

'Tis the business of little minds to shrink, but they whose heart is firm, and whose conscience approves their conduct, will pursue their principles unto death.

—Leonardo da Vinci

The Crooked Road of Success

How are these for excuses?

50 percent of businesses fail in the first 5 years.[6]

40 to 50 percent of married couples in the United States divorce.[7]

The average cost of raising a child to 18 years of age in the United States is $245,340.[8]

Does having the "facts" mean you never try?

No. Millions of people every year are brave or stupid enough to believe they will be the ones who succeed.

The roads of success in business, marriage and raising children are long, complex and always crooked. You advance, get knocked down, get going again, plateau, go backwards and sideways. You are surprised by the direction you are taking and where you end up. At any time you can decide that where you are is the end point—that it is all you can achieve. That you are as happy and successful as you will be.

Have you noticed that the words "gratitude" and "resilience" haven't been mentioned much in this book about being brave? Why? You can get through a situation and gratefully return to your prior set point for happiness and actually decide not to be brave enough to try again—to continue down the crooked road of success.

You can be grateful and resilient and still decide not to pursue your dreams.

Imagine that as your life.

Well, I could not and cannot.

Is it easy to keep traveling on the road to your dreams? No. The only thing that carries you through is love, and love is not easy. But love from others is easier when you love yourself first. On that foundation, loving what you do, who you do it with and having the support and love of those you love determines whether or not you continue to live your dash with all your heart.

The only thing that carries you through is love, and love is not easy.

3 F's of Success

Focus

Follow Up

Follow Through

Brave or Stupid?

 In 2006, when my husband was 72 years old, we decided to buy our second hotel. It was big. It was beautiful. It was set in the picturesque town of Prescott, Arizona.

I can still remember the October day in 2003 when, as we made the turn onto Highway 69, we saw it for the first time. We had set out from Cottonwood, Arizona to buy supplies for our first hotel acquisition. We both commented on the hotel and I remember saying, "I could own that hotel." Richard agreed and immediately began doing some research.

When you're 72, have one business that is just breaking even, a child in college and a mortgage on your house, never ask your financial planner if you should buy another business which would require your spouse to cut back on her income-producing business. The cold stare and questioning of your intelligence may be too much.

But it was a risk we both wanted to take. We acquired the property for under book value. We had the operational expertise to execute its growth potential; we had a strong balance sheet, and the economy was booming. On paper we knew we could make it work because we were willing to work at it. We knew the business. We liked the business, and Richard loved managing employees almost as much as he loved me.

We were focused, we followed up and we followed through. By 2008 we were within the top 5% in customer satisfaction for the brand; we had attracted an incredible staff; we had 100% occupancy in October; and we had won an award for community involvement.

And then we learned that when theory meets application, the outcome may still not meet your goals. Because in November 2008 recession hit the hotel business hard. We gave our hotel back to the bank. Our dreams for our future were abruptly halted; our strong balance sheet was on life support; and my consulting business was all but nonexistent.

What did we have? The ability to forgive ourselves. The ability to trust in ourselves and each other. The knowledge that excuses would not help us reach our goal. And love. Lots and lots of love. That's why we were brave, not stupid.

Rites of Passage

Overcoming adversity and, ultimately, denying it the rite of passage, has been a constant and perpetual motive throughout my life.

—Heather Mills

My only child celebrated her 30th birthday by ushering many new experiences into her life. The interesting part of her celebration for me was that I began to receive lots of inquiries about my emotional state! As her birthday approached, many who have known me during the last 30 years wondered if I was sad, or panicked, or sorrowful. I was surprised at the inquiries. In fact, looking back, my emotional state was downright gleeful.

Having been a child when the slogan "don't trust anyone over 30" came into fashion, I had unconsciously viewed one's 30th birthday as the real rite of passage into adulthood. Of course, 18 and 21 have legal merit and every young adult looks forward (as I did) to those life markers as "the point" to prove they are now adults. From what I can tell, those rites of passage allow you to test how wrong you really are about life. At 18, you can leave home, pile up debt, get married, drive, vote, go to war and, in most countries, drink alcohol, without asking permission. At 21, it is harder to find someone else who is legally responsible for any of those things you were allowed to do at 18.

Thirty, on the other hand, is no longer about asking permission or having others potentially being responsible for your decisions. At 30, not only do those younger than you think you no longer understand them, but you get to take all the responsibility for everything you do. And no one cares if you asked permission or not.

You see, that was all part of why I was gleeful when my daughter, Dana, turned 30. I knew it was opening the way for my next 30 years. I would continue to care more deeply for her than I ever thought possible, but I was gaining a level of healthy detachment from the outcomes. My responsibility was now totally centered in my "respons-i-bility." I would no longer waste time on shame. I would no longer blame myself. I would no longer have a need to rationalize. I would simply look back on the crooked road paved with the story of my life and see the acts of bravery that gave me just enough inspiration to decide to dream again.

The ability to dream again is the real rite of passage. You see, the ability to dream again, be brave again, and love again, is never guaranteed, but must always be assumed.

Even when you do things the right way, you may not get to where you thought you should be. Whether it is the long journey to love yourself, or the ability to love your child through the period when they love very little about you, or the shifts in your love when you walk through the loss of your dreams, remember that forgiving and trusting will always be the brave choices. They will always be right.

Forgiving and trusting will always be the brave choices.

Why? Because love will always be right. Before I learned that lesson, I made every excuse. I taught every lesson I needed to learn more than once, and I now have enough experience to know that I always had what I wanted and didn't even know it. You see, at a very young age, I was taught that love was all you need. I just took a very crooked road to get to where I really believe that message and make it central to my life.

. . . love will always be right

Uncle Louie

A flower cannot blossom without sunshine, and man cannot live without love.

—Max Muller

 Are you old enough to remember the sound of a rotary dial phone ringing? When phones sat on a desk or were mounted on a wall and you only had one choice of what the ringtone sounded like?

One of my first great achievements as a child was being able to reach the phone to answer it. As the youngest and only girl in our one-phone-in-the-hallway family, it was a big deal to be first to the phone and get to answer it. I always raced to get it.

Now if you can imagine that, imagine this.

Each night, usually 15 minutes before my father got home from his long, arduous day which started at the Fulton Meat Market and ended as he locked the door to his butcher shop in Flatbush, the phone would ring.

If I happened to be the first one to get to the phone for this daily call, within seconds my face turned sour and my Mom was there to grab the phone from my hand.

It took a few years for me to learn to check the clock that hung prominently in the kitchen, in clear view from where the phone hung 15 feet away. The just-before-7 call wasn't one I wanted to answer. You see, if it was just before 7 p.m. and just before Dad got home, I would know who was on the other end. I also knew I was now old enough that my Mom wasn't going to take the phone—or my discomfort—away. Instead, if I answered the call, I would experience the uneasy desire to end the call as soon as possible.

As exciting as the sound of the phone ringing was, I developed a lot of anxiety around the sounds I heard when I answered that call. Usually I would hear a human grunt of some form. Enough to know it was Uncle Louie calling. And the conversation usually went like this:

Grunt.

"Hi, Uncle Louie. Dad isn't here."

What happened next was not as predictable. Sometimes it would be a slow sound I could tell was disappointment. Other times, it would be a sound of irritation or urgency.

All the time, all I wanted to happen was for the call to end.

———•◆•———

I was probably in my mid-to-late twenties before I came to realize how much those calls, and Uncle Louie himself, shaped my life and my belief in what is possible when there is love and a refusal to accept how things are.

Here is the deal with Uncle Louie. Like me, he was one of the last children in a big family. He was near the end of the line of 11 kids. My father's family. He was born in 1928 with severe Down's syndrome. As was the practice at that time, the family was told to sign my uncle over to the state so he would be housed by that authority in an institution. The family was also told to expect he would live no more than one year.

What happened instead of that dire scenario taught me as much about responsibility and love as any other lesson I've ever learned. The family flatly refused. They not only flatly refused, they took their baby home and began the process of ignoring what he could *not* do and *would never* do, and they focused on the fact that he was a part of their family and would be treated just like everyone else.

So what did that mean? It meant he was at every dinner table; he was spoken to as though he was as capable of under standing as anyone else in the family. As Uncle Louie got older all his brothers wore suits to work every day, so Uncle Louie wore a suit every day. Even though Uncle Louie never developed the ability to speak, he was fully understood. Although he could never dial a phone by himself, he would walk to a corner candy store each day, with a pocket full of coins and a list of his brothers' and sisters' phone numbers, and with the help of the shop owner or a local patron, he called each of his married siblings every night.

He not only lived one year; he lived 53.

He never learned to speak, but he knew how to communicate.

He never got out of diapers, but he wore suits and a pinky ring.

When he died, one of the most remarkable, glorious scenes unfolded. This man—a man who could never really have a conversation—had touched so many hearts the funeral parlor line overflowed to the street. No one came to tell a story of what a burden it had been to the family, because having Uncle Louie was not seen as a burden. On the contrary:

Everyone had a story about what Uncle Louie meant to them and how he impacted their life and made their life better.

He hadn't had a career or made a cent in his life, but his life had been a success.

A success made of love given and love passed on, proving that love is the ultimate success.

Change your awareness and your perspective changes.

On the morning of September 7, 2015, as I was finalizing this manuscript, I synchronistically received this email from TUT.com (aka The Universe Talks), a service that delivers a daily inspirational message.

From: The Universe [mailto:theuniverse@tut.ccsend
.com] On Behalf Of The Universe
Sent: Monday, September 7, 2015 12:56 AM
To: drsuccess@servingsuccess.com
Subject: TUT - A Note from the Universe

True brilliance, Andrea, is not a function of understanding one's view of the world and finding order, logic, and spirituality in it. True brilliance is understanding that your view of order, logic, and spirituality is what created your world.

And therefore being forever capable of changing everything.

The Universe

Being brave means you create the world you want to live in. Don't die waiting to be brave.

Don't Die™ Books Postscript

By design, *Don't Die* books share the stories of real people, living real lives that continue on after the snapshot of time each book captures—just as my life has evolved since I began writing this book. Each book connects synchronistic moments; and toward the end of the writing process, the people at the center of each of the other *Don't Die* books touched my life again. Synchronistic moments, of course, are not all pleasant. Pleasant or not, in their synchronicity they confirm the concept that we are all one. It is our "oneness" that helps each of us find the strength to live, love and prosper again.

Don't Die with Vacation Time on the Books began with Marel Giolito imploring me to make her promise not to die with vacation time on the books. Since that book was published, Marel has taken many vacations, including a romantic honeymoon. She successfully sold her business and has been called once again to find the strength to live through a health crisis. I can't predict the outcome, but in the meantime I know she is living, loving and prospering from the love of others as she bravely faces this newest challenge.

A magical 31-day period in the life of Gary Russo inspired *Don't Die with Your Song Unsung.* In the years following the publication of the book, Gary continued singing and making people smile. As is true to all lives, Gary (like Marel) also continued to face great challenges at a personal and professional level. On or about July 29, 2015—four years to the day that the first video of Gary's lunchtime performances was randomly posted on You-Tube—Gary forgot that we were all connected, that he was not alone, and that he could overcome life's challenges yet again. In that moment of darkness, Gary took his own life.

In death, as in life, Gary will continue to be a great inspiration and a great teacher to me.

———•◆•———

I will not die an unlived life.
I will not live in fear
of falling or catching fire.
I choose to inhabit my days,
to allow my living to open me,
to make me less afraid,
more accessible;
to loosen my heart
until it becomes a wing,
a torch, a promise.
I choose to risk my significance,
to live so that which came to me as seed
goes to the next as blossom,
and that which came to me as blossom,
goes on as fruit.

—Dawna Markova[*]

[*]I WILL NOT DIE AN UNLIVED LIFE ©2000 by Dawna Markova, used with permission from Red Wheel Weiser, LLC Newburyport, MA and San Francisco, CA, www.redwheelweiser.com.

You Are Brave Enough Journal

Don't Die Waiting to Be Brave, the third book in the *Don't Die* series, is about being brave enough to love yourself enough to finally go after what you want out of life. To recognize that your life really matters, that who and how you love really matters, and that you are successful. When you take the step to say all this about your life, you will have proven to yourself that you are brave!

That is it in a nutshell. Your bravery. Your life. Your loves. Your success.

I have taken you for a walk on my crooked road of success using the *Don't Die* Principles. Now it's your turn to prove to yourself that you have been brave enough, you are brave enough, and you are willing to be brave enough again.

Change your awareness and

What synchronistic events have come into my awareness?

_____

_____

_____

_____

_____

_____

_____

_____

_____

_____

_____

_____

_____

_____

_____

_____

_____

_____

your perspective changes.

What challenges or tragedies could I reframe as gifts?

_____

_____

_____

_____

_____

_____

_____

_____

_____

_____

_____

_____

_____

_____

_____

_____

_____

_____

_____

You teach what

What lesson have I been taught that I need to learn again now?

you need to learn.

Have I found my voice? Do I mind my voice?

_____

_____

_____

_____

_____

_____

_____

_____

_____

_____

_____

_____

_____

_____

_____

_____

_____

_____

You can make excuses or you can achieve

Where do I want to be more brave in my life?

_____

_____

_____

_____

_____

_____

_____

_____

_____

_____

_____

_____

_____

_____

_____

_____

_____

your goals, but you can't do both.

What is truly holding me back from being brave enough?

_____

_____

_____

_____

_____

_____

_____

_____

_____

_____

_____

_____

_____

_____

_____

_____

_____

_____

Experience is what you get when

What "best worst decision" have I ever made?

_____

_____

_____

_____

_____

_____

_____

_____

_____

_____

_____

_____

_____

_____

_____

_____

_____

_____

you don't get what you want.

If experience is "what you get when you did not
get what you wanted," what do I want?

_____

_____

_____

_____

_____

_____

_____

_____

_____

_____

_____

_____

_____

_____

_____

An Invitation for You to Write Your Own Don't Die™ Story

http://www.LivingTheSpirit.Today

Since creating the *Don't Die* brand in 2010, I've met countless people who have a compelling Living the Spirit story to tell. Many thought I would want to write their story, but I said no. As a trained professional in the field of personal development and psychology, I know that research tells me not to. Writing is an integral part of human development and a critical tool in personal development.

Just as no one else can live your life, no one else can write your human development story for you. You must do it yourself. For this reason, I offer you an invitation to write your own story.

Go to www.LivingTheSpirit.Today, where there are guidelines to help you along. Write away. This is your chance to look back on your crooked road of success so that you can begin to build a path to move forward.

If you choose to upload your story, it may be edited and shared, in whole or in part, to inspire others under the guidelines of Creative Commons (CC).*

We all have our own stories, and we are connected in oneness . . .

---

*A Creative Commons (CC) license is one of several public copyright licenses that enable the free distribution of an otherwise copyrighted work. A CC license is used when an author wants to give people the right to share, use, and build upon a work that they have created. All submissions on www.LivingTheSpirit.Today will be governed by Creative Commons (CC).

Quotations

What step would I take today if I were brave?

—Jana Stanfield

Being brave doesn't mean you can't feel afraid. It means you have the courage to step beyond your fears and do it anyway.

—Cathy Pagano

Keeping the questions alive doesn't mean deciding what's true. It just means keeping the conversation engaged.

—Elizabeth Lloyd Mayer

Many people die with their music still in them. Why is this so? Too often it is because they are always getting ready to live. Before they know it, time runs out.

—Oliver Wendell Holmes, Sr.

Die to the past every moment. You don't need it. Only refer to it when it is absolutely relevant to the present. Feel the power of this moment and the fullness of Being.

—Echart Tolle

Courage is what it takes to stand up and speak; courage is also what it takes to sit down and listen.

—Winston Churchill

"...focusing on whatever we dislike empowers it."

—Ellen Debenport

Trust is the first step to love.

—Munshi Premchand

When marrying, ask yourself this question: Do you believe that you will be able to converse well with this person into your old age? Everything else in marriage is transitory.

—Friedrich Nietzsche

Your children are not your children. They are the sons and daughters of Life's longing for itself. They came through you but not from you and though they are with you yet they belong not to you.

—Khalil Gibran

'Tis the business of little minds to shrink, but they whose heart is firm, and whose conscience approves their conduct, will pursue their principles unto death.

—Leonardo da Vinci

Overcoming adversity and, ultimately, denying it the rite of passage, has been a constant and perpetual motive throughout my life.

—Heather Mills

A flower cannot blossom without sunshine, and man cannot live without love.

—Max Muller

To live in hearts we leave behind is not to die.

—Thomas Campbell

Notes

1. K. Nance, "Scott Simon on 'Unforgettable,'" *Chicago Tribune*, April 30, 2015

2. M. Csikszentmihalyi, *Flow: The Psychology of Optimal Experience* (New York: HarperCollins, 1990), p. 4

3. http://www.brainyquote.com/quotes/topics/topic _forgiveness .html#7cokl2jbEh8J6j91.99

4. Composite definition of *experience*, Oxford American Dictionary, Heald Colleges Edition, 1980

5. http://www.brainyquote.com/quotes/quotes/m /munshiprem184048.html#MKbv6A0OID3q7oUS.99

6. U.S. Department of Labor, Bureau of Labor Statistics, Business Employment Dynamics, "Entrepreneurship and the U.S. Economy" http://www.bls.gov/bdm /entrepreneurship/entrepreneurship.htm

7. Adapted from *Encyclopedia of Psychology* (2000), quoted in American Psychological Association "Marriage & Divorce," www.apa.org/topics/divorce/

8. M. Lino, Expenditures on Children by Families, 2013. U.S. Department of Agriculture, Center for Nutrition Policy and Promotion. Miscellaneous Publication No. 1528-2013, http://www.cnpp.usda.gov/sites/default/files/expenditures_on _children_by_families/crc2013.pdf

The Don't Die™ Book Series

The crooked road of success is paved with books. What better way to traverse the potholes and curves of life success than to use the advice they offer? The *Don't Die* series is just part of a collection of personal development products from ServingSuccess (www.ServingSuccess.com) designed to help you achieve your goals. Each *Don't Die* book offers guidance for developing a personal roadmap of life success.

In each book, Dr. Success™ (aka Dr. Andrea Goeglein) curates real stories of life journeys that inspire you to create action plans for your personal growth. Topics include psychological and spiritual transformation, transforming your life into a positive force, and the mystery of money, happiness and love. *Don't Die* books are about living life with a spirit that will not die no matter what life throws your way. A *Don't Die* spirit is the positive energy you create from not only surviving troubling or traumatic life events, but also from striving to live fully again. The stories told in each book are constructed around the four *Don't Die* Principles of personal responsibility:

Change your awareness and your perspective changes.

You teach what you need to learn.

You can make excuses or you can achieve your goals, but you can't do both.

Experience is what you get when you don't get what you want.

Don't Die books form a "small books, big impact" series: small size so that you can read one in 45 minutes, big impact because that brevity gives you time to consider your own real-life *Don't Die* story by working with the journal in the last section of each book.

Inspiration plus action: that's what *Don't Die* books deliver.

———— •◆• ————

Don't Die with Vacation Time on the Books

Don't Die with Your Song Unsung (with Gary Russo)

Don't Die Waiting to Be Brave

Through agreement with Hay House Publishing, Don't Die™ was licensed for their publication:

Don't Die with Your Music Still in You (Serena J. Dyer and Dr. Wayne W. Dyer)

About the Author

Dr. Andrea Goeglein is an expert in the application of Positive Psychology to daily life, goal attainment and overall life success. She earned her doctoral degree in organizational psychology after achieving significant success in business endeavors that included owning hotels. Now she is devoted to bringing the tenets of Positive Psychology to life for her clients and audiences.

Guided by the principles of love, learning and prosperity, Dr. Goeglein has been a counselor and personal mentor to the CEOs of privately held companies. She has capitalized on her talents as a dynamic national speaker, major event organizer, community activist, author and business consultant to build a powerful portfolio of personal development services.

A much sought-after media personality known as "Dr. Success," Dr. Goeglein frequently appeared as an expert guest on KAZ-TV's AM Arizona; she has also appeared on the Rachael Ray show and on major radio networks across the nation.

Through her Dr. Success™ blog, Andrea is a Success Sherpa. She carries and delivers information that feeds minds and touches hearts.

Her interviews, writings and sightings can be viewed at:

www.ServingSuccess.com/blog
https://twitter.com/DrSuccess
https://www.youtube.com/user/ServingSuccess
www.ServingSuccess.com
www.DontDieBooks.com
https://www.facebook.com/DrSuccessPhD

Working with the Author

Through her company ServingSuccess, Dr. Andrea Goeglein offers a wide range of personal development services that will help you and your organization apply Positive Psychology to daily life, business goal attainment and overall life success.

In addition to working one-on-one with select executive clients, Dr. Goeglein offers inspirational group learning experiences which include:

- ◆ invitation-only entrepreneurial success groups
- ◆ executive women's telegroups
- ◆ teleclasses, teleseminars, *Don't Die*™ writing workshops and other day-long gatherings
- ◆ video sharing
- ◆ books

Dr. Goeglein is an independent Everything DiSC® Authorized Partner.* The Everything DiSC® Workplace Profile is a behavioral instrument that allows you to learn about you. There is no better place to start to raise your personal level of self-awareness. The online version gives you immediate delivery of your profile for a minimal investment of your time (10 minutes) and money.

---

*Everything DiSC® is a registered trademark of John Wiley & Sons, Inc.

More information about ServingSuccess's offerings can be found at http://www.Serving Success.com. To initiate a personal dialogue with Dr. Goeglein to discuss how you or your organization can work with her, call 1-866-975-3777 or write DrSuccess@ServingSuccess.com

Create Your Own Don't Die™ Spirit Living Library

Pass this book on to someone else and encourage
them to do the same when they have finished reading it.

Name of Giver	Date	Gifted to

If you would like to share your true *Don't Die* spirit story, go to
www.LivingTheSpirit.Today

8/16

NS